SCIENTIFIC
FACTS
IN THE
BIBLE

RAY COMFORT

Newberry, FL 32669

Scientific Facts in the Bible

Bridge-Logos, Inc.
Newberry, FL 32669, USA

Edited by Lynn Copeland

Cover, page design, and production by Genesis Group

Cartoons by Richard Gunther

Unless otherwise indicated, Scripture quotations are from the New King James version, © 1979, 1980, 1982 by Thomas Nelson Inc., Publishers, Nashville, Tennessee.

ISBN 978-0-88270-879-9

Library of Congress Control Number: 2001095148

Printed in India

Contents

Introduction

I Hope You Are Skeptical

"Suppose I believed that I was God and that I thought the whole universe revolved around me?" The confident youth waited for my reaction to his question. I simply answered, "I think that you would be a *normal* human being." He was a little taken aback that I wasn't impressed by his "outrageous" statement, and asked, "What do you mean?" I explained by asking him where he thought "here" was. He told me that it was where *he* stood.

Every human being thinks that same way. We define "here" as being where *we* are. Everything and everyone else is "there." Each of us thinks that we are the center of the universe. Semantics? Let's take it a little further. Define "now" for me. Tell me *when* it is. You can't. The split second that you try to pinpoint "now," it becomes "then." I often find myself explaining the nature of "now" after I ask people if they have ever stolen something. This is their typical answer to the question: "Yes, I have. But that was in the past." I explain to them that *everything* is in the "past." You are even forced to define the reading of this sentence as something you did *in the past*.

These thoughts are a little strange, and you may be thinking that there are some things that we *can*

3

still be sure of—the sun still rises, the sky is still blue, and "up" is still "up." Not true. The sun never rises. The earth turns, giving us the illusion that the sun is rising, although it remains still (it *seems* to be still, but it is actually moving through the universe). The sky *isn't* blue. Ask any astronaut. It has no color. Neither is "up" up. Remember that the earth is round. What is up to someone at the North Pole is not up to someone at the South Pole. In fact, if everyone on the earth pointed to where we thought was "up," we would all point in different directions.

So many things that we think are absolutes are not. History has shown us that even what science defines as truth today may be laughed at in one hundred years.

What then can we be sure of? Is there such a thing as "absolute," unchanging truth? We will look at this subject later in this publication.

In April 2001, through a series of strange circumstances, I found myself speaking at the American Atheists, Inc., National Convention in Orlando, Florida. The audience of 250 were reasonably polite... until I made the statement that the Bible was filled with scientific and medical facts, written thousands of years before man discovered them. The reaction was one of immediate and unified mockery.

Their response was understandable. If I was speaking the truth, then the Bible is supernatural in origin —not a pleasant thought for a professing atheist. This, however, is not altogether bad news for the unbeliever. If the Bible *proves* itself to be the Word of the One who created all things, it would make sense to search its pages. After all, time will take each of us to the grave, and if there was one chance in a million that the Bible's promise of immortality and threat of damnation is true, we owe it to our good sense just to look into it.

The Bible doesn't attempt to defend its inspiration. Genesis simply opens with the words "God said." It repeats these words nine times in the first chapter. The phrase "The LORD spoke" is used 560 times in the first five books of the Bible and at least 3,800 times in the whole of the Old Testament. Isaiah claims at least 40 times that his message came directly from God; Ezekiel, 60 times; and Jeremiah, 100 times.

There are about 3,856 verses directly or indirectly concerned with prophecy in Scripture. Mormons, Buddhists, and Muslims have what they consider their own sacred writings, but the element of proven prophecy is absent in them. Neither do any other books in any of the world's religions (Vedas, Bhagavad-Gita, Koran, etc.) contain scientific truth. In fact, they contain statements that are clearly unscientific.

Most people are not aware that the Bible was written over a period of 1,600 years, by more than 40 authors, who wrote on three different continents in three different languages. They spoke on hundreds of controversial subjects, and yet they penned their words with agreement and harmony.

These facts make the information given in this publication even more incredible.

Before we look at these "scientific facts" in the Bible, I must preface them with some very important information. To do this, I will have to quote the Bible. This is not using what is commonly called "circular reasoning." I simply want to make a point that is relevant to what I am going to present.

Many years ago, I ran a children's club. At the end of the club I told about one hundred kids to line up for some candy. There was an immediate rush, and the line sorted itself into what I saw as being a line of greed. The bigger, selfish kids were at the front, and the small and timid ones were at the back. I then did something that gave me great satisfaction. I told the kids to turn about face. Everyone did. Then I told them to stay where they were, and I took great delight in going to the other end of the line and giving the candy to the smaller, timid kids first.

In a world where the rich and powerful often take advantage of the poor and meek, we are informed that God has gone to the other end of the line with the message of everlasting life (I know that you may not believe in the existence of God, but please bear with me). Here is what we are told:

> For the message of the cross is foolishness to those who are perishing...For it is written: "I will destroy the wisdom of the wise, and bring to nothing the understanding of the prudent." ...But God has chosen the foolish things of the world to put to shame the wise, and God has chosen the weak things of the world to put to shame the things which are mighty; and the base things of the world and the things which are despised God has chosen, and the things which

are not, to bring to nothing the things that are, that no flesh should glory in His presence. (1 Corinthians 1:18,19,27–29)

How has God gone to the other end of the line? Simply by choosing that which is foolish, weak, base, and despised. Let me illustrate what He has done.

Do you believe that the following biblical accounts actually happened?

- Adam and Eve
- Noah's ark
- Jonah and the whale
- Joshua and the walls of Jericho
- Samson and his long hair
- Daniel and the lion's den
- Moses and the Red Sea

If you're an atheist, of course you don't. To you, believing such fantastic stories would mean that you would have to surrender your intellectual dignity. Who in their right mind would ever do that? The answer is simply *those who understand that God has chosen foolish, weak, base, and despised things of the world to confound those who think they are wise.*

Consider the intellectual offense in the tone of this letter I received, prior to a debate I had on the subject "Does God exist?":

How sad for you to have so completely surrendered your intellect to an ignorant, pre-scientific book. I know about your upcoming debate... I won't be there, but I'm sure that the audience will get some good belly laughs from your presentation. Biblical literalists may not be very bright, but they are extremely funny.

I hope you have opened this book with a good deal of skepticism. You should. The world is full of simple folk who will make a shrine to a knot in a tree because it supposedly has the features of a dead "saint." You are wise to consider the evidence before deciding whether something is true.

Where's the Evidence?

Imagine that you are viewing a luxury liner moving through calm waters. To your amazement, about a dozen people jump off the ship and cling to a lifeboat. You watch as the rest of the passengers stand on the ship and laugh at them. You can understand their reaction. What those few people did was foolish. *It made no sense.*

Suddenly, the ship hits an unseen iceberg and sinks, taking with it all who stayed on board. Now you see that those who seemed like fools were wise, but those who stayed on the ship and seemed to be wise were fools.

We have in the Bible a command to jump off the luxury liner of this world. Before you laugh at stupid Christians, ask yourself if there is any proof that its claims are true. The following pages give compelling evidence that the Bible is no ordinary book.

1

Science and the Bible

The Bible and Earth's Free-float in Space

At a time when some believed that the earth sat on a large animal or a giant (1500 BC), the Bible spoke of the earth's free float in space: "He hangs the earth on nothing" (Job 26:7). Science didn't discover that the earth hangs on nothing until 1650.

The Scriptures Speak of an Invisible Structure

Only in recent years has science discovered that everything we see is composed of things that we cannot see—invisible atoms. In Hebrews 11:3, written 2,000 years ago, Scripture tells us that the "things which are seen were not made of things which are visible."

The Bible Reveals that the Earth is Round

The Scriptures tell us that the earth is round: "It is He who sits above the circle of the earth" (Isaiah 40:22).

The word translated "circle" here is the Hebrew word *chuwg,* which is also translated "circuit" or "compass" (depending on the context). That is, it indicates something spherical, rounded, or arched—not something that is flat. The book of Isaiah was written sometime

 between 740 and 680 BC. This is at least 300 years before Aristotle suggested, in his book *On the Heavens,* that the earth might be a sphere. It was another 2,000 years later (at a time when science believed that the earth was flat) that the Scriptures inspired Christopher Columbus to sail around the world.

The Bible and the Science of Oceanography
Matthew Maury (1806–1873) is considered the father of oceanography. He noticed the expression "paths of the sea" in Psalm 8:8 (written 2,800 years ago) and said, "If God said there are paths in the sea, I am going to find them." Maury then took God at His word and went looking for these paths, and we are indebted to his discovery of the warm and cold continental currents. His vital book on oceanography is still in print today.

The Bible and Radio Waves
God asked Job a very strange question in 1500 BC. He asked, "Can you send out lightnings, that they may go, and say to you, 'Here we are!'?" (Job 38:35).

This appears to be a scientifically ludicrous statement—that light can be *sent*, and then manifest itself in speech. But did you know that all electromagnetic radiation—from radio waves to X-rays—travels at the speed of light? This is why you can have *instantaneous* wireless communication with someone on the other side of the earth. The fact that light could be sent and then manifest itself in speech wasn't discovered by science until 1864 (3,300 years later), when "British scientist James Clerk Maxwell suggested that electricity and light waves were two forms of the same thing" (*Modern Century Illustrated Encyclopedia*).

The Bible and Entropy
Three different places in the Bible (Isaiah 51:6; Psalm 102:25,26; and Hebrews 1:11) indicate that the earth is wearing out like a garment. This is what the Second Law of Thermodynamics (the Law of Increasing Entropy) states: that in all physical processes, every ordered system over time tends to become more disordered. Everything is running down and wearing out as energy is becoming less and less available for use. That means the universe will eventually "wear out" to the extent that (theoretically speaking) there will be a "heat death" and therefore no more energy available for use. This wasn't discovered by science until recently, but the Bible states it in concise terms.

The Bible and the Water Cycle
The Scriptures inform us, "All the rivers run into the sea, yet the sea is not full; to the place from which the

rivers come, there they return again" (Ecclesiastes 1:7). This statement alone may not seem profound. But, when considered with other biblical passages, it becomes all the more remarkable. For example, the Mississippi River dumps approximately 518 billion gallons of water every 24 hours into the Gulf of Mexico. Where does all that water go? And that's just one of thousands of rivers. The answer lies in the hydrologic cycle, so well brought out in the Bible.

Psalm 135:7 tells us, "He causes the vapors to ascend from the ends of the earth; He makes lightning for the rain." Ecclesiastes 11:3 states that "if the

clouds are full of rain, they empty themselves upon the earth." Look at the Bible's concise words in Amos 9:6: "He...calls for the waters of the sea, and pours them out on the face of the earth." The idea of a complete water cycle was not fully understood by science until the seventeenth century. However, more than two thousand years prior to the discoveries of Pierre Perrault, Edme Mariotte, Edmund Halley, and others, the Scriptures clearly spoke of a water cycle.

The Bible and the First Law of Thermodynamics

The Scriptures say, "Thus the heavens and the earth, and all the host of them, were finished" (Genesis 2:1). The original Hebrew uses the past definite tense for the verb "finished," indicating an action completed in the past, never again to occur. The creation was "finished"—once and for all. That is exactly what the First Law of Thermodynamics says. This law (often referred to as the Law of the Conservation of Energy and/or Mass) states that neither matter nor energy can be either created or destroyed.

It was because of this Law that Sir Fred Hoyle's "Steady-State" (or "Continuous Creation") Theory was discarded. Hoyle believed that at points in the universe called "irtrons," matter (or energy) was constantly being created. But, the First Law states just the opposite. Indeed, there is no "creation" ongoing today. It is "finished" exactly as the Bible states.

The Bible and Ship Dimensions
In Genesis 6, God gave Noah the dimensions of the 1.5 million cubic foot ark he was to build. In 1609 at Hoorn in Holland, a ship was built after that same pattern (30:5:3), revolutionizing shipbuilding. By 1900 every large ship on the high seas was in-clined toward the proportions of the ark (verified by "Lloyd's Register of Shipping" in the *World Almanac*).

The Bible and Meteorological Laws
The Scriptures describe a "cycle" of air currents two thousand years before scientists discovered them: "The wind goes toward the south, and turns around to the

north; the wind whirls about continually, and comes again on its circuit" (Ecclesiastes 1:6). We now know that air around the earth turns in huge circles, clockwise in one hemisphere and counterclockwise in the other.

The Bible and Science

"In antiquity and in what is called the Dark Ages, men did not know what they now know about humanity and the cosmos. They did not know the lock  but they possessed they key, which is God. Now many have excellent descriptions of the lock, but they have lost the key. The proper solution is union between religion and science. We should be owners of the lock *and* the key. The fact is that as science advances, it discovers what was said thousands of years ago in the Bible." —Richard Wurmbrand, *Proofs of God's Existence*

2

The Incredible Book of Job

Book of Job (1520 BC)—Filled with Scientific Facts

"The study of the Book of Job and its comparison with the latest scientific discoveries has brought me to the matured conviction that the Bible is an inspired book and was written by the One who made the stars."
—Charles Burckhalter, Chabot Observatory

The Book of Job and the Earth's Rotation

For ages, scientists believed in a geocentric view of the universe. The differences between night and day were believed to be caused by the sun revolving around the earth. Today, we know that the earth's rotation on its axis is responsible for the sun's rising and setting. But around 3,500 years ago, it was written, "Have

 you commanded the morning since your days began, and caused the dawn to know its place? ... It [the earth] takes on form like clay under a seal" (Job 38:12,14). The Hebrew word for "takes on form"

means "to turn," and alludes to the rolling cylindrical seal used to stamp an impression on clay—an accurate analogy of the earth's rotation.

The Book of Job and Springs of the Sea

"Modern deep-sea-diving cameras have discovered amazing hot-water vents on the floor of the oceans— 'the springs of the sea,' which are mentioned in Job 38:16. These thermal vents release huge amounts of mineral-rich, super-heated water." —Richard Gunther

"There are four main points in this matter that the Old Testament affirms. First, the Old Testament asserts positively that springs do exist in the ocean [Job 38:16]. The source of this knowledge claims omniscience and is allowing that omniscience to be tested by scientific investigation of the ocean floor. Second, the undersea springs are said to have been established at the earth's creation [Psa. 33:6,7]. Third, the Flood of Noah is claimed to have been caused, at least in part, by an unusual activity of ocean floor springs [Gen. 7:11]. Finally, springs are mentioned so we can marvel at the wisdom and power of God [Prov. 8:22,28]." —Steven A. Austin, PhD

The Book of Job and the Way of Light

Job 38:19 asks, "Where is the way to the dwelling of light?" Modern man has only recently discovered that light (electromagnetic radiation) has a "way." In empty space this speed is approximately 186,000 miles per second.

The Book of Job and Dinosaurs

Why did dinosaurs disappear? Science can only speculate. However, the answer may be in Job 40:15–24. In this passage, God Himself speaks of a great creature called "behemoth." Some Bible commentators think this is a reference to the hippopotamus. However, one of the characteristics of this massive animal is that it had a tail the size of a large tree. The hippo's tail isn't like a tree; it's more like a small twig.

Here are all the given characteristics of this huge animal: It was the largest of all the creatures God made, was plant-eating (herbivorous), had tremendous strength in its hips and a tail like a large tree. It had bones as strong as bronze and iron, lived among the trees, drank massive amounts of water,  and was not disturbed by a raging river. He appears impervious to attack because his nose could pierce through snares, but Scripture says, "Only He who made him can bring near His sword" (v. 19). Perhaps God caused this, the largest of all the creatures He had made, to become extinct.

3

Medical Science and the Bible

The Bible and Laws of Hygiene

Encyclopedia Britannica documents that in 1845, a young doctor in Vienna named Dr. Ignaz Semmelweis was horrified at the terrible death rate of women who gave birth in hospitals. As many as 30 percent died after childbirth. Semmelweis noted that doctors would examine the bodies of patients who died, then, without washing their hands, go straight to the next ward and examine expectant mothers. This was their normal practice, because the presence of microscopic diseases was unknown.

Semmelweis insisted that doctors wash their hands before each examination, and the death rate immediately dropped to 2 percent.

 Look at the specific instructions God gave thousands of years ago to His people for when they encountered disease: "And when he who has a discharge is cleansed of his discharge, then he shall count for himself seven

days for his cleansing, wash his clothes, and bathe his body in running water; then he shall be clean" (Leviticus 15:13). Until recent years, doctors washed their hands in a bowl of water, leaving invisible germs on their hands. However, the Bible says specifically to wash under "running water."

The Bible and the Immune System

The Bible instructs that male babies are to be circumcised on the *eighth* day (Genesis 17:12). Medical science has now discovered that this is the day that the coagulating factor in the blood, called prothrombin, is the highest. It reaches its peak on the eighth day, then drops. Medical science has also discovered that this is when the  human body's immune system is at its peak.

The Bible and the Correlation of Mind and Body

Medical science has come to understand that there is a strong relationship between a person's mental and physical health. The Bible revealed this to us with these statements (and others) written around 950 BC:

- "A sound heart is life to the body, but envy is rottenness to the bones" (Proverbs 14:30).

- "The light of the eyes rejoices the heart, and a good report makes the bones healthy" (Proverbs 15:30).

- "Pleasant words are like a honeycomb, sweetness to the soul and health to the bones" (Proverbs 16:24).

- "A merry heart does good, like medicine, but a broken spirit dries the bones" (Proverbs 17:22).

The Bible and Laws of Quarantine

Long before medical science discovered the importance of quarantining persons with infectious diseases, the Bible instructed it. In 1490 BC the Scriptures tell the people of Israel what to do if someone has a skin condition like leprosy: "All the days he has the sore he shall be unclean. He is unclean, and he shall dwell alone; his dwelling shall be outside the camp" (Leviticus 13:46).

Laws of quarantine were not instigated by modern man until the seventeenth century.

"During the devastating Black Death of the fourteenth century, patients who were sick or dead were kept in the same rooms as the rest of the family. People often wondered why the disease was affecting so many people at one time. They attributed these epidemics to 'bad air' or 'evil spirits.' However, careful attention to the medical commands of God as revealed in Leviticus would have saved untold millions of lives. Arturo Castiglione wrote about the overwhelming importance of this biblical medical

21

law: 'The laws against leprosy in Leviticus 13 may be regarded as the first model of sanitary legislation' (*A History of Medicine*)." —Grant R. Jeffery, *The Signature of God*

4

Science and Genesis

Scientists Admit Genesis is "Close to the Truth"
Scientists get a little nervous when they realize that their discoveries lead them back to Genesis chapter 1. Notice the use of the word "uncanny" in the following quotes:

"Most cosmologists (scientists who study the structures and evolution of the universe) agree that the Genesis account of creation, in imagining an initial void, may be uncannily close to the truth."
—*Time* (December 1976)

"The universe suddenly exploded into being... The big bang bears an uncanny resemblance to the Genesis command." —Jim Holt, *Wall Street Journal* science writer

"New scientific revelations about supernovas, black holes, quarks, and the big bang even suggest to some scientists that there is a 'grand design' in the universe." —*U.S. News & World Report* (March 31, 1997)

The Bible Speaks of a Specific Design

"Slight variations in physical laws such as gravity or electromagnetism would make life impossible...The necessity to produce life lies at the center of the universe's whole machinery and design." —John Wheeler, Princeton University professor of physics (*Reader's Digest*, September 1986)

Even evolutionist *Stephen Hawking*, considered the best-known scientist since Albert Einstein, acknowledges "the universe and the laws of physics seem to have been specifically designed for us. If any one of about 40 physical qualities had more than slightly different values, life as we know it could not exist: Either atoms would not be stable, or they wouldn't combine into molecules, or the stars wouldn't form the heavier elements, or the universe would collapse before life could develop, and so on..." —*Austin American Statesman* (October 19, 1997)

Genesis and the Universe

Science expresses the universe in five terms: time, space, matter, power, and motion. Genesis 1:1,2 perfectly revealed such truths to the Hebrews in 1450 BC: "In the beginning *[time]* God created *[power]* the heavens *[space]* and the earth *[matter]*...And

the Spirit of God was hovering *[motion]* over the face of the waters." The first thing God tells man is that He controls all aspects of the universe.

The Bible Speaks of One Common Ancestor

"Researchers suggest that virtually all modern men—99% of them, says one scientist—are closely related genetically and share genes with one male ancestor, dubbed 'Y-chromosome Adam.' We are finding that humans have very, very shallow genetic roots which go back very recently to one ancestor... That indicates that there was an origin in a specific location on the globe, and then it spread out from there." —*U.S. News & World Report* (December 4, 1995)

The Bible and the Universal Flood

"It takes special conditions to make a fossil, and the world is covered with billions of them in mass graves. Creatures must be buried rapidly before they rot or get eaten by scavengers. And, in fact, vast numbers of animals were buried and fossilized so quickly that some could not even finish swallowing their meal or giving birth. We find fossils of sea creatures in rock layers that cover all the continents. For example, most of the rock layers in the walls of Grand Canyon (more than a mile above sea level) contain marine fossils. Fossilized shellfish are even found in the Himalayas.

"Another obvious evidence is fossils of tree trunks standing upright or upside down through more than one layer. This doesn't make sense with the slow accumulation of layers over millions of years, but instead it is a sign that these polystrate fossils were buried rapidly.

"Another obvious example is rock layers that were deposited around the globe at the same time. For example, the Tapeats Sandstone, which sits on the basement rocks of Grand Canyon (Arizona), also appears far away in Wisconsin and across the ocean in Israel and Libya (under different names).

"You can go to many places on the planet and see row upon row of consecutively deposited rock layers that were soft when deposited and then bent, sometimes drastically. The whole series shows no signs of fracturing. Obviously, hard rocks do not bend without breaking. A better explanation is that the Flood laid these layers rapidly, and they were bent before they could dry out and harden." —Answers in Genesis

Law of Probabilities Confirms Genesis

"The chance that higher life forms might have emerged in this way [through evolution] is comparable to the chance that a tornado sweeping through a junkyard might assemble a Boeing 747 from the materials therein."

"The likelihood of the formation of life from inanimate matter is one out of $10^{40,000}$...It is big enough to bury Darwin and the whole theory of evolution. There was no primeval soup, neither on this planet nor on any other, and if the beginnings of life were not random, they must therefore have been the product of purposeful intelligence." —Sir Fred Hoyle, professor of astronomy, Cambridge University

Genesis Explains the Origin of Sexes

Almost all forms of complex life have both male and female—horses, dogs, humans, moths, monkeys, fish, elephants, birds, etc. The male needs the female to reproduce, and the female needs the male to reproduce. One cannot carry on life without the other. The Bible tells us that "He who made them at the beginning 'made them male and female'" (Matthew 19:4). But if evolution were true, which then came first according to the theory?

If a male came into being before a female, how did the male of each species reproduce without females? How is it possible that a male and a female each spontaneously came into being, yet they have complex, complementary reproductive systems? If each sex was able to reproduce without the other, why (and how) would they have developed a reproductive system that requires both sexes in order for the species to survive?

Genesis Differentiates Man from the Animals

The Bible tells us that animals are created "without understanding." Human beings are different from animals. We are made in God's "image." We aren't merely a higher form of species on the evolutionary scale. As human beings, we are aware of our "being." God is "I AM," and we know that "we are." We have understanding that we exist. Among other unique characteristics, we have an innate ability to appreciate God's creation. What animal gazes with awe at a sunset, or at the magnificence of the Grand Canyon? What animal obtains joy from the sounds of music or takes the time to form itself into an orchestra to create and harmonize music? We are also moral beings. What animal among the beasts sets up court systems and apportions justice to its fellow creatures?

While birds and other creatures have instincts to create (nests, etc.), we have the ability to uncover the hidden laws of electricity. We can utilize the law of aerodynamics to transport ourselves around the globe. We also have the God-given ability to appreciate the *value* of creation. We unearth the hidden treasures of gold, silver, diamonds, and oil and make use of them for our own benefit. Only humans have the unique ability to appreciate God for this incredible creation and to respond to His love.

5

Scientists and the Bible

Scientists Who Believed the Bible

"Most of the great scientists of the past who founded and developed the key disciplines of science were creationists. Note the following sampling:

Physics: Newton, Faraday, Maxwell, Kelvin

Chemistry: Boyle, Dalton, Pascal, Ramsay

Biology: Ray, Linnaeus, Mendel, Pasteur

Geology: Steno, Woodward, Brewster, Agassiz

Astronomy: Kepler, Galileo,[1] Herschel, Maunder

"These men, as well as scores of others who could be mentioned, were creationists, not evolutionists, and their names are practically synonymous with the rise of modern science. To them, the scientific enterprise was a high calling, one dedicated to 'thinking God's thoughts after Him.'" —Henry M. Morris and Gary E. Parker, *What Is Creation Science?*

---

[1] It was the Roman Catholic church that opposed Galileo, not the Christian Church.

Harvey (1578–1657), Boyle (1627–1691), Faraday (1791–1867), and Maxwell (1831–1879) were all committed Christians. Boyle (the first scientist to show the difference between compounds and elements) was a lay preacher. Faraday (the discoverer of electromagnetic induction) once read only from the Bible for a sermon, saying his words could add nothing to God's. Maxwell (who discovered magnetic flux) penned these words: "Lord, it belongs not to my care, whether I die or live. To love and serve Thee is my share, and that Thy guard must give."

Astronomer Johann Kepler believed, "The chief aim of all investigation of the external world should be to discover the rational order and harmony which has been imposed on it by God."

Lord Kelvin wrote, "With regard to the origin of life, science . . . positively affirms creative power."

Much of modern scientific knowledge is built on the discoveries of other Bible-believing scientists:

- Leonardo Da Vinci (1452–1519): Experimental science, physics
- Francis Bacon (1561–1626): Scientific method
- Samuel F. B. Morse (1791–1872): Telegraph
- William Petty (1623–1687): Statistics, scientific economics
- William Derham (1657–1735): Ecology

- James Joule (1818–1889): Thermodynamics
- Henri Fabre (1823–1915): Entomology of living insects
- Joseph Henry (1797–1878): Electric motor, galvanometer

Arthur H. Compton

Arthur H. Compton, winner of the Nobel Prize in Physics, stated: "Science is the glimpse of God's purpose in nature. The very existence of the amazing world of the atom and radiation points to a purposeful creation, to the idea that there is a God and an intelligent purpose back of everything...An orderly universe testifies to the greatest statement ever uttered: 'In the beginning, God...'"

Sir Isaac Newton

Sir Isaac Newton (1642–1662) considered his theological writings more important than his scientific writings. He stated, "There is a Being who made all things, who holds all things in His power, and is therefore to be feared."

He also wrote, "All material things seem to have been composed of the hard and solid particles abovementioned, variously associated in the first creation by the counsel of an intelligent Agent. For it became Him who created them to set them in order. And if He did so, it's unphilosophical to seek for any other origin of the world, or to pretend that it might arise out of a chaos by the mere laws of nature."

Joseph Lister

Joseph Lister (1827–1912) founded antiseptic surgical methods. Lister's contributions to medical science have probably led to more lives being saved through modern medicine than the contributions of anyone else except Pasteur. Like Louis Pasteur, Lister was a Christian. He wrote, "I am a believer in the fundamental doctrines of Christianity."

Blaise Pascal

Blaise Pascal (1623–1662) was one of history's greatest mathematicians. He laid the foundations for hydrostatics, hydrodynamics, differential calculus, and the theory of probability. He is famous for the "Wager of Pascal," paraphrased as follows:

> How can anyone lose who chooses to be a Christian? If, when he dies, there turns out to be no God and his faith was in vain, he has lost nothing—in fact, has been happier in life than his non-believing friends. If, however, there is a God and a heaven and hell, then he has gained heaven and his skeptical friends will have lost everything in hell!

Sir John Frederick Herschel

Sir John Frederick Herschel, an English astronomer who discovered over 500 stars, stated: "All human discoveries seem to be made only for the purpose of confirming more and more strongly the truths that come from on high and are contained in the Sacred Writings."

His father, Sir William Herschel, also a renowned astronomer, rightly insisted, "The undevout astronomer must be mad."

Albert Einstein

Albert Einstein was not an atheist as some professing atheists claim. He didn't accept the God of the Bible, but he wasn't a fool. He knew that there was a Creator. Look at his words about faith and science:

Science can only be created by those who are thoroughly imbued with the aspiration toward truth and understanding. This source of feeling, however, springs from the sphere of religion. To this there also belongs the faith in the possibility that the regulations valid for the world of existence are rational, that is, comprehensible to reason. I cannot conceive of a genuine scientist without that profound faith.

James Simpson

Dr. James Simpson, born in 1811, was responsible for the discovery of chloroform's anesthetic qualities, leading to its medical use worldwide. He also laid a solid foundation for gynecology and predicted the discovery of the X-ray. Dr. Simpson was president of the Royal Medical Society and Royal Physician to the Queen, the highest medical position of his day. He stated, "Christianity works because it is supremely true and therefore supremely livable. There is nothing incompatible between religion and science."

When asked what his greatest discovery was, Dr. Simpson replied: "It was not chloroform. It was to know I am a sinner and that I could be saved by the grace of God. A man has missed the whole meaning of life if he has not entered into an active, living relationship with God through Christ."

6

Biology and the Bible

The Bible and Plant Life

Plants need sunlight, water, and minerals in order to grow and to make their own energy and food. If plants do not get sunlight, and yet have water and minerals, they cannot produce chlorophyll. They will then die. It is interesting to notice therefore the chronological order of the Genesis creation. God created light first (Genesis 1:3). He then created water (v. 6), then soil (v. 9), and *then* He created plant life (v. 11).

Bible Statements Consistent With Biology

The great biological truth concerning the importance of blood in our body's mechanism has been fully comprehended only in recent years. Until about 130 years ago, sick people were "bled," and many died because of the practice. If you lose your blood, you lose your life. The reason doctors give a "blood test" is because blood carries an incredible amount of information about the health of the flesh. The Book of Leviticus, written in 1400 BC, declared that blood is the source of life: "For the life of the flesh is in the blood" (17:11). The blood carries water and nourishment to every cell, maintains the body's temperature, and removes the waste material of the body's cells. It also carries oxygen from the lungs throughout the body. In 1616, William Harvey discovered that blood circulation is the key factor in physical life—confirming what the Bible revealed 3,000 years earlier.

Blood is far more complex and has far more to do with life than science ever imagined. About 55 percent of the blood is composed of plasma. The rest is  made of three major types of cells: red blood cells (also known as erythrocytes), white blood cells (leukocytes), and platelets (thrombocytes). Plasma consists predominantly of water and salts. The kidneys carefully maintain the salt concentration in plasma because small changes in its concentration will cause cells in the body to function improperly. In extreme conditions this can result in death.

Look at how the blood affects the flesh: Antibodies in the blood neutralize or help destroy infectious organisms. Each antibody is designed to target one specific invading organism. For example, chicken pox antibody will target chicken pox virus, but will leave an influenza virus unharmed. There is no better way to describe the function of blood in relation to the human body than to say, "The life of the flesh is in the blood."

The Bible and Biogenesis

The theory of evolution requires that nonliving chemicals somehow developed completely by chance into highly complex, living organisms. However, nonliving things coming to life is the stuff of science fiction, not science. Louis Pasteur's famous and repeatable experiments have demonstrated the Law of Biogenesis: that "spontaneous generation" is impossible and that life can arise only from other life. The Scriptures describe biogenesis—that God is the Creator of life, and that each creature reproduces its own kind (humankind, dog kind, cat kind, etc.); nothing evolves to become any new kind of creature:

- "And the LORD God formed man of the dust of the ground, and breathed into his nostrils the breath of life; and man became a living being" (Genesis 2:7).

- "Then God said, 'Let the earth bring forth grass, the herb that yields seed, and the fruit tree that yields fruit according to its kind, whose seed is in itself, on the earth'; and it was so. And the earth brought forth grass, the herb that yields seed according to its kind, and the tree that yields fruit, whose seed is in itself according to its kind. And God saw that it was good" (Genesis 1:11,12).

- "So God created great sea creatures and every living thing that moves, with which the waters abounded, according to their kind, and every winged bird according to its kind. And God saw that it was good" (Genesis 1:21).

37

- "And God made the beast of the earth according to its kind, cattle according to its kind, and everything that creeps on the earth according to its kind. And God saw that it was good" (Genesis 1:25).

The phrase "according to its kind" occurs repeatedly, stressing the reproductive integrity of each kind of animal and plant. Today we understand that this occurs because all of these reproductive systems are programmed by their genetic codes.

"Natural Kinds" Validate the Bible

"This notion of species as 'natural kinds' fits splendidly with creationist tenets of a pre-Darwinian age. Louis Agassiz even argued that species are God's individual thoughts, made incarnate so that we might perceive both His majesty and His message. Species, Agassiz wrote, are 'instituted by the Divine Intelligence as the categories of his mode of thinking.' But how could a division of the organic world into discrete entities be justified by an evolutionary theory that proclaimed ceaseless change as the fundamental fact of nature?" —Stephen J. Gould, professor of geology and paleontology, Harvard University

7

The Bible's 100% Accurate Prophecies

The Scriptures and Fulfilled Prophecies
Prophecies from the Old and New Testaments that have been fulfilled also add credibility to the Bible. The Scriptures predicted the rise and fall of great empires like Greece and Rome (Daniel 2:39,40), and foretold the destruction of cities like Tyre and Sidon (Isaiah 23). Tyre's demise is recorded by ancient historians, who tell how Alexander the Great lay siege to the city for seven months. King Nebuchadnezzar of Babylon had failed in his 13-year attempt to capture the seacoast city and completely destroy its inhabitants.

During the siege of 573 BC, much of the population of Tyre moved to its new island home approximately half a mile off the coast. Here it remained surrounded by walls as high as 150 feet until judgment fell in 332 BC with the arrival of Alexander the Great. In the seven-month siege, he fulfilled the remainder of the prophecies (Zechariah 9:4; Ezekiel 26:12) concerning the city at sea by completely destroying Tyre, killing 8,000 of its inhabitants and selling 30,000 of its population into slavery. To reach the island, he scraped up the dust and rubble of the old land city of Tyre, just like the Bible predicted, and cast it into the sea, building a 200-foot-wide causeway out to the island. Alexander's death and the murder of his two sons were also foretold in the Scripture.

Another startling prophecy was Jesus' detailed prediction of Jerusalem's destruction, and the further dispersion of the Jewish people throughout the world, which is recorded in Luke 21. In AD 70, not only was Jerusalem destroyed by Titus, the future emperor of Rome, but another prediction of Jesus Christ (Matthew 24:1,2) came to pass—the complete destruction of the Jerusalem temple.

The Bible's Prediction of the Middle East Conflict

In Genesis, the Book of Beginnings, God said that Ishmael (the progenitor of the Arab race; see *Time*, April 4, 1988) would be a "wild man...and every man's hand [will be] against him. And he shall dwell in the presence of all his brethren" (Genesis 16:12). Almost four thousand years later, who could deny that this prophecy is being fulfilled in the Arab race? The Arabs and the Jews are "brethren" having Abraham as their ancestor. The whole Middle East conflict is caused by their dwelling together.

The Bible's Messianic Prophecies

The Old Testament prophets declared that the one and only Messiah would, among many other things, be born in Bethlehem (Micah 5:2) to a virgin (Isaiah 7:14), be betrayed for thirty pieces of silver (Zechariah 11:12,13), die by crucifixion (Psalm 22), and be buried in a rich man's tomb (Isaiah 53:9)—all prior to the temple's demise in AD 70. There was only one person who fits all of the messianic prophecies of the Old Testament: Jesus of Nazareth, the Son of Mary.

The scientific probability that any one person could fulfill just eight of these prophecies is 1 in 10^{17}. But in all, there are over three hundred prophecies that tell of the ancestry, birth, life, ministry, death, resurrection, and ascension of Jesus of Nazareth. All have been literally fulfilled to the smallest detail.

The Bible Predicted the Birth of a Nation

In Isaiah 66:8 (700 BC), the prophet gives a strange prophecy: "Shall the earth be made to give birth in one day? Or shall a nation be born at once? For as soon as Zion was in labor, she gave birth to her children." In 1922 the League of Nations gave Great Britain the mandate (political authority) over Palestine. On May 14, 1948, Britain withdrew her mandate, and the nation of Israel was "born in a day."

There are more than twenty-five Bible prophecies concerning Palestine that have been literally fulfilled.

Probability estimations conclude that the chances of these being randomly fulfilled are less than one chance in 33 million.

Signs of the Times Verify the Bible

There will be false Christs; wars and rumors of wars; nation rising against nation; famines; disease (pestilence); false prophets who will deceive many; and lawlessness (forsaking of the Ten Commandments). The gospel will be preached in all the world. There will be earthquakes in various places; signs from heaven (in the sun, moon, and stars); and persecution against Christians in all nations. Men's hearts will fail them

for fear of the future; they will be selfish, materialistic, arrogant, proud. Homosexuality will increase; there will be blasphemy; coldheartedness; intemperance; brutality; rebellious youth; hatred of those who stand up for righteousness; ungodliness; pleasure-seeking; much hypocrisy. False Bible teachers will have many followers, be money-hungry, and slander the Christian faith (see 2 Peter 2:1–3).

Men will scoff and say that there was no such thing as the flood of Noah and that these "signs" have always been around. Their motivation for hating the truth will be their love of lust (2 Peter 3:1–7). The Scriptures tell us that they make one big mistake. Their understanding of God is erroneous. They don't understand that God's time frame is not the same as ours. They think (in their ignorance) that God's continued silence means that He doesn't see their sins. In truth, He is merely holding back His wrath, waiting for them to repent and escape the damnation of hell.

Jesus warned that the sign to look for was the repossession of Jerusalem by the Jews. That happened in 1967, after 2,000 years, bringing into culmination all the signs of the times. (These are combined from Matthew 24; Mark 13; Luke 21; 1 Timothy 4; and 2 Timothy 3.)

The Bible Predicts Russia's Attack of Israel

A number of books of the Bible speak of future events. Ezekiel 38 (written approximately 600 BC) prophesies that in these times ("the latter days," v. 16), Russia (referred to as the "Prince of Rosh"; see *Smith's Bible Dictionary*, p. 584) will combine with Iran, Libya (in Hebrew called "Put"), and Ethiopia (in Hebrew called "Cush") and attack Israel (vv. 5–8). This will take place after an Israeli peace initiative has been successful (v. 11).

The Bible even gives the Russian reasoning for and the direction of the attack (vv. 10–15), as well as the location of the battle (Armageddon—Revelation 16:16). This is generally interpreted as meaning "the mountain of Megiddo," which is located on the north side of the plains of Jezreel. Russia has had a foothold in the Middle East for many years: "The Soviets are entrenched around the rim of the Middle East heartland, in Afghanistan, South Yemen, Ethiopia, and Libya." —"Countdown in the Middle East," *Reader's Digest* (May 1982)

The Bible and Armageddon

Joel 2:1–10 relates a striking account of the coming Battle of Armageddon, the greatest of all battles. As this vision (which seems to entail flame-throwing tank warfare) was given to him approximately 2,800 years ago, the prophet relates it to the only thing he has seen in battle—horse-drawn chariots. Think of modern warfare and compare: fire goes before them (v. 3); they burn what is behind them (v. 3); they destroy everything in their path (v. 3); they move at the speed of a horse (30–40 mph, v. 4); their rumbling sounds like the noise of many chariots and the roar of a fire (v. 5); they climb over walls (v. 7); they don't break ranks (v. 7); the sword can't stop them (v. 8); they climb into houses (v. 9); and they make the earth quake (v. 10).

The Bible and Nuclear War

Ezekiel 39, written over 2,500 years ago, speaks of God's judgment upon the enemies of Israel. Verses 12–15 describe what will happen after what many see as the Battle of Armageddon:

> "For seven months the house of Israel will be burying them, in order to cleanse the land… They will set apart men regularly employed, with the help of a search party, to pass through the land and bury those bodies remaining on the ground, in order to cleanse it. At the end of seven

months they will make a search. The search party will pass through the land; and when anyone sees a man's bone, he shall set up a marker by it, till the buriers have buried it in the Valley of Hamon Gog."

Before the days of nuclear warfare, this portion of the Bible would have made no sense to the reader. We are told that even the weapons left by the enemy will have to be burned (Ezekiel 39:9). So many will die that it will take those specially employed for the purpose seven months to bury the dead (v. 14). The Scriptures are very specific about the method of burial. When even a bone is found by searchers, a special marker is to be placed near the bone until the buriers have buried it. This would seem to be a clear reference to radioactive contamination after nuclear war. This thought is confirmed in Joel 2:30, which speaks of "pillars of smoke."

The Book of Peter and Nuclear Weapons

The Bible suggests the effects of nuclear weaponry. This is certainly not something that could have been explained in AD 67 using known scientific principles (when Peter wrote the following verse):

But the day of the Lord will come as a thief in the night, in which the heavens will pass away with a great noise, and the elements will melt with fervent heat; both the earth and the works that are in it will be burned up (2 Peter 3:10).

8

Astronomy and the Bible

The Bible and "Lights"

God created the "lights" in the heavens "for signs and seasons, and for days and years" (Genesis 1:14). Through the marvels of astronomy we now understand that a year is the time required for the earth to travel once around the sun. The seasons are caused by the changing position of the earth in relation to the sun—"astronomers can tell exactly from the earth's motion around the sun when one season ends and the next one begins" (*Worldbook Multimedia Encyclopedia*). We also now understand that a "month [is] the time of one revolution of the moon around the earth with respect to the sun" (*Encyclopedia Britannica*). How could Moses (the accepted author of Genesis) have known 3,500 years ago that the "lights" of the sun and moon were the actual determining factors of the year's length, unless his words were inspired by God?

The Bible and the Stars

In Jeremiah 33:22, the Bible states that "the host of heaven cannot be numbered, nor the sand of the sea measured." When this was written, 2,500 years ago, no one knew how vast the stars were, as fewer than 1,100 were visible. Now we know that there are *billions* of stars, and that they *cannot* be numbered.

The Bible also tells us that each star is unique (1 Corinthians 15:41). All stars look alike to the naked  eye. Even when seen through a telescope, they still seem to be just points of light. However, close examination of their light spectra reveals that each is different from all others.

The Bible and the Revolving Earth

The Scriptures tell us that the Second Coming of Jesus Christ (which will happen at the speed of light —Luke 17:24) will occur while some are asleep at night and others are working at daytime activities in the field. This is a clear indication of a revolving earth, with day and night at the same time. Science didn't discover this until the fifteenth century.

The Bible and the Sun's Circuit

In speaking of the sun, the psalmist (800 BC) said, "Its rising is from one end of heaven, and its circuit to the other end; and there is nothing hidden from its heat" (Psalm 19:6). For many years critics scoffed at this verse, claiming that it taught the doctrine of geocentricity (i.e., the sun revolves around the earth). Scientists at that time thought the sun was stationary. However, it has been discovered in recent years that the sun is in fact moving through space at approximately 600,000 miles per hour. It is traveling through the heavens and has a "circuit" just as the Bible says. Its circuit is so large that it would take approximately 200 million years to complete one orbit.

The Bible and the Expanding Universe

At least seven times in Scripture we are told that God "stretches out the heavens like a curtain" (e.g., Isaiah 40:22). It wasn't until the 1920s that astronomers observed evidence that galaxies are moving away from each other, indicating the entire universe is expanding, or stretching out—a fact that the Bible spoke of thousands of years earlier.

Astronomy Confirms the Bible

In 1964, Drs. Arno Penzias and Robert Wilson of Bell Labs discovered a noise coming from all directions, permeating the universe. Physicists hailed this as the first observational evidence of the Big Bang known as "the radio echo of creation."

Penzias saw the philosophical significance in his discovery. "[T]he best data we have," he said, "are exactly what I would have predicted, had I had nothing to go on but the five books of Moses, the Psalms, the Bible as a whole... [T]he creation of the universe is supported by all the observable data astronomy has produced so far."

9

Historical Figures and the Bible

Sir Isaac Newton Believed the Bible

Sir Isaac Newton, the father of modern science, said these wise words: "We account the Scriptures of God to be the most sublime philosophy. I find more sure marks of authenticity in the Bible than in any profane history whatsoever."

Samuel Morse Believed the Bible

Samuel Morse, famous for his invention of the telegraph, gave God the glory for his inventions. It is fitting that the first message he ever sent over the wire was taken from Scripture: "What hath God wrought!" (Numbers 23:23). Morse wrote these words four years before he died: "The nearer I approach the end of my pilgrimage, the clearer is the evidence of the divine origin of the Bible. The grandeur and sublimity of God's remedy for fallen man are more appreciated and the future is illuminated with hope and joy."

Theodore Roosevelt Believed the Bible

"No educated man can afford to be ignorant of the Bible."

"A thorough knowledge of the Bible is worth more than a college education."

Napoleon Believed the Bible

"The Bible is no mere book, but a Living Creature, with a power that conquers all that oppose it...I never omit to read it, and every day with new pleasure." Napoleon also wrote about Jesus:

> I know men and I tell you that Jesus Christ is no mere man. Between Him and every other person in the world there is no possible term of comparison. Alexander, Caesar, Charlemagne, and I have founded empires. But on what did we rest the creations of our genius? Upon force. Jesus Christ founded His empire upon love; and at this hour millions of men would die for Him.

Patrick Henry Believed the Bible

"Here is a Book worth more than all the other books which were ever printed; yet it is my misfortune never to have, till lately, found time to read it with proper intention or feeling."

Andrew Jackson Believed the Bible

"That book, Sir, is the Rock upon which our republic rests."

William McKinley Believed the Bible

"The more profoundly we study this wonderful Book, and the more closely we observe its divine precepts, the better citizens we will become and the higher will be our destiny as a nation."

Woodrow Wilson Believed the Bible

"There are a good many problems before the American people today, and before me as President, but I expect to find the solution of those problems just in the proportion that I am faithful in the study of the Word of God."

Thomas Jefferson Believed the Bible

"I have always said, and always will say, that the studious perusal of the Sacred Volume will make us better citizens, better fathers and better husbands."

Herbert Hoover Believed the Bible

"The whole inspiration of our civilization springs from the teachings of Christ and the lessons of the prophets. To read the Bible for these fundamentals is a necessity of American life."

John Quincy Adams Believed the Bible

"I say to you, Search the Scriptures! The Bible is the book of all others, to be read at all ages, and in all conditions of human life; not to be read once or twice or thrice through, and then laid aside, but to be read in small portions of one or two chapters every day, and never to be intermitted, unless by some overruling necessity."

Franklin D. Roosevelt Believed the Bible

"We cannot read the history of our rise and development as a nation, without reckoning the place the Bible has occupied in shaping the advances of the Republic."

"It is a fountain of strength and now, as always, an aid in attaining the highest aspirations of the human soul."

Ulysses S. Grant Believed the Bible

"Hold fast to the Bible as the sheet anchor of your liberties; write its precepts in your hearts, and practice them in your lives."

Charles Dickens Believed the Bible

"The New Testament is the very best book that ever was or ever will be known in the world."

Sir Winston Churchill Believed the Bible

"Let men of science and learning expound their knowledge and prize and probe with their researches every detail of the records which have been preserved to us from those dim ages. All they will do is fortify the grand simplicity and essential accuracy of

the recorded truths which have lighted so far the pilgrimage of men."

John Adams Believed the Bible
"The Bible is the best book in the world. It contains more than all the libraries I have seen."

"Suppose a nation in some distant region should take the Bible for their only law book, and every member should regulate his conduct by the precepts there exhibited! Every member would be obligated in conscience, to temperance, frugality, and industry; to justice, kindness, and charity towards his fellow men; and to  piety, love, and reverence toward Almighty God... What a Utopia, what a paradise would this region be."

Ronald Reagan Believed the Bible
"Within the covers of the Bible are all the answers for all the problems men face. The Bible can touch hearts, order minds and refresh souls."

George Washington Believed the Bible
Washington had private devotions, both morning and evening, during which he was seen in a kneeling position with a Bible open before him, as was his daily practice.

"Direct my thoughts, words, and work. Wash away my sins in the immaculate Blood of the Lamb, and purge my heart by Thy Holy Spirit . . . Daily frame me more and more into the likeness of Thy Son Jesus Christ."

"It is the duty of all nations to acknowledge the Providence of Almighty God, to obey His will, to be grateful for His benefits, and humbly to implore His protection and favor."

Daniel Webster Believed the Bible

"I have read the Bible through many times, and now make it a practice to read it through once every year. It is a book of all others for lawyers, as well as divines; and I pity the man who cannot find in it a rich supply of thought and of rules for conduct. It fits a man for life—it prepares him for death."

"If we abide by the principles taught in the Bible, our country will go on prospering."

Noah Webster Believed the Bible

"The moral principles and precepts contained in the Scriptures ought to form the basis of all our civil constitutions and laws. All the miseries and evils which men suffer from—vice, crime, ambition, injustice, oppression, slavery, and war—proceed from their despising or neglecting the precepts contained in the Bible."

Dwight Eisenhower Believed the Bible

"The Bible is endorsed by the ages. Our civilization is built upon its words. In no other Book is there such a collection of inspired wisdom, reality, and hope."

"It takes no brains to be an atheist. Any stupid person can deny the existence of a supernatural power because man's physical senses cannot detect it. But there cannot be ignored the influence of conscience, the respect we feel for the Moral Law, the mystery of first life...or the marvelous order in which the universe moves about us on this earth. All these evidence the handiwork of the beneficent Deity...That Deity is the God of the Bible and Jesus Christ, His Son."

Albert Schweitzer Believed the Bible

"We must all mutually share in the knowledge that our existence only attains its true value when we have experienced in ourselves the truth of the declaration: 'He who loses his life shall find it.'"

Calvin Coolidge Believed the Bible

"The foundations of our society and our government rest so much on the teachings of the Bible that it would be difficult to support them if faith in these teachings would cease to be practically universal in our country."

Christopher Columbus Believed the Bible

"It was the Lord who put it into my mind...I could feel His hand upon me...There is no question the inspiration was from the Holy Spirit because He comforted me with rays of marvelous illumination from the Holy Scriptures…" (from his diary, in reference to his discovery of "the New World").

General Robert E. Lee Believed the Bible
"There are things in the old Book which I may not be able to explain, but I fully accept it as the infallible Word of God, and receive its teachings as inspired by the Holy Spirit."

"In all my perplexities and distresses, the Bible has never failed to give me light and strength."

Abraham Lincoln Believed the Bible
"I believe the Bible is the best gift God has given to man."

He also said, in declaring a day of national fasting, prayer, and humiliation in 1863: "Whereas, it is the duty of nations as well as of men to own their dependence upon the overruling power if God, to confess their sins and transgressions in humble sorrow yet with assured hope that genuine repentance will lead to mercy and pardon, and to recognize the sublime truth, announced in the Holy Scriptures and proven by all history: that those nations only are blessed whose God is the Lord…

"We have been the recipients of the choicest bounties of Heaven. We have been preserved these many years in peace and prosperity. We have grown in numbers, wealth and power as no other nation has ever grown. But we have forgotten

God. We have forgotten the gracious Hand which preserved us in peace, and multiplied and enriched and strengthened us; and we have vainly imagined, in the deceitfulness of our hearts, that all these blessings were produced by some superior wisdom and virtue of our own.

"Intoxicated with unbroken success, we have become too self-sufficient to feel the necessity of redeeming and preserving grace, too proud to pray to the God that made us!

"It behooves us then to humble ourselves before the offended Power, to confess our national sins and to pray for clemency and forgiveness."

Congress and the Bible

The Bible is the Word of God according to the United States Congress. In a joint resolution requesting the President proclaim 1983 as the "Year of the Bible," it declared:

> ...the Bible, the Word of God, has made a unique contribution in shaping the United States as a distinctive and blessed nation and people... Deeply held religious convictions springing from the Holy Scriptures led to the early settlement of our nation... Biblical teachings inspired concepts of civil government that are contained in our Declaration of Independence and the Constitution of the United States (Public Law 97-280).

10

Archaeology and the Bible

Archaeology and History Attest to the Bible
By Richard M. Fales, Ph.D.
No other ancient book is questioned or maligned like the Bible. Critics looking for the flyspeck in the masterpiece allege that there was a long span between the time the events in the New Testament occurred and when they were recorded. They claim another gap exists archaeologically between the earliest copies made and the autographs of the New Testament. In reality, the alleged spaces and so-called gaps exist only in the minds of the critics.

Manuscript Evidence. Aristotle's *Ode to Poetics* was written between 384 and 322 BC. The earliest copy of this work dates AD 1100, and there are only forty-nine extant manuscripts. The gap between the original writing and the earliest copy is 1,400 years. There are only seven extant manuscripts of Plato's Tetralogies, written 427–347 BC. The earliest copy is AD 900—a gap of over 1,200 years. What about the New Testament? Jesus was crucified in AD 30. The New Testament was written between AD 48 and 95.

The oldest manuscripts date to the last quarter of the first century, and the second oldest AD 125. This gives us a narrow gap of thirty-five to forty years from the originals written by the apostles. From the early centuries, we have some 5,300 Greek manuscripts of the New Testament. Altogether, including Syriac, Latin, Coptic, and Aramaic, we have a whopping 24,633 texts of the ancient New Testament to confirm the

 wording of the Scriptures. So the bottom line is, there was no great period between the events of the New Testament and the New Testament writings. Nor is there a great time lapse between the original writings and the oldest copies.

With the great body of manuscript evidence, it can be proved, beyond a doubt, that the New Testament says exactly the same things today as it originally did nearly 2,000 years ago.

Corroborating Writings. Critics also charge that there are no ancient writings about Jesus outside the New Testament. This is another ridiculous claim. Writings confirming His birth, ministry, death, and resurrection include Flavius Josephus (AD 93), the Babylonian Talmud (AD 70–200), Pliny the Younger's letter to the Emperor Trajan (approx. AD 100), the Annals of Tacitus (AD 115–117), Mara Bar Serapion (sometime after AD 73), and Suetonius' *Life of Claudius* and *Life of Nero* (AD 120).

Another point of contention arises when Bible critics have knowingly or unknowingly misled people by implying that Old and New Testament books were either excluded from or added into the canon of Scripture at the great ecumenical councils of AD 336, 382, 397, and 419. In fact, one result of these gatherings was to confirm the Church's belief that the books already in the Bible were divinely inspired. Therefore, the Church, at these meetings, neither added to nor took away from the books of the Bible. At that time, the thirty-nine Old Testament books had already been accepted, and the New Testament, as it was written, simply grew up with the ancient Church. Each document, being accepted as it was penned in the first century, was then passed on to Christians of the next century. So, this foolishness about the Roman Emperor Constantine dropping books from the Bible is simply uneducated rumor.

The Dead Sea Scrolls Bear Out the Bible
By William F. Albright

The discovery of the Dead Sea Scrolls (DSS) at Qumran [in 1947] had significant effects in corroborating evidence for the Scriptures. The ancient texts, found hidden in pots in cliff-top caves by a monastic religious community, confirm the reliability of the Old Testament text. These texts, which were copied and studied by the Essenes, include one complete Old Testament book (Isaiah) and thousands of fragments, representing every Old Testament book except Esther.

The manuscripts date from the third century BC to the first century AD and give the earliest window found so far into the texts of the Old Testament books and their predictive prophecies. The Qumran texts have become an important witness for the divine origin of the Bible, providing further evidence against the criticism of such crucial books as Daniel and Isaiah.

Dating the Manuscripts. Carbon-14 dating is a reliable form of scientific dating when applied to uncontaminated material several thousand years old. Results indicated an age of 1917 years with a 200-year (10 percent) variant. Paleography (ancient writing forms) and orthography (spelling) indicated that some manuscripts were inscribed before 100 BC. Albright set the date of the complete Isaiah scroll to around 100 BC—"there can happily not be the slightest doubt in the world about the genuineness of the manuscript."

Archaeological Dating. Collaborative evidence for an early date came from archaeology. Pottery accompanying the manuscripts was late Hellenistic (c. 150–63 BC) and Early Roman (c. 63 BC to AD 100). Coins found in the monastery ruins proved by their inscriptions to have been minted between 135 BC and AD 135. The weave and pattern of the cloth supported an early date. There is no reasonable doubt that the Qumran manuscripts came from the century before Christ and the first century AD.

Significance of the Dating. Previous to the DSS, the earliest known manuscript of the Old Testament was the Masoretic Text (AD 900) and two others (dating about AD 1000) from which, for example, the King James version of the Old Testament derived its translation. Perhaps most would have considered the Masoretic text as a very late text and therefore questioned the reliability of the Old Testament wholesale. The Dead Sea Scrolls eclipse these texts by 1,000 years and provide little reason to question their reliability, and further, present only confidence for the text. The beauty of the Dead Sea Scrolls lies in the close match they have with the Masoretic text—demonstrable evidence of reliability and preservation of the authentic text through the centuries. So the discovery of the DSS provides evidence for the following:

1) Confirmation of the Hebrew Text

2) Support for the Masoretic Text

3) Support for the Greek translation of the Hebrew Text (the Septuagint). Since the New Testament often quotes from the Greek Old Testament, the DSS furnish the reader with further confidence for the Masoretic texts in this area where it can be tested.
—"Dead Sea Scrolls," adapted from Norman Geisler, *Baker Encyclopedia of Christian Apologetics*

Modern Archaeology Confirms the Bible

"In extraordinary ways, modern archeology is affirming the historical core of the Old and New Testaments, supporting key portions of crucial biblical stories."
—Jeffery L. Sheler, "Is the Bible True?" *Reader's Digest* (June 2000)

Archaeological Discoveries and the Bible
"Archaeology has confirmed countless passages which have been rejected by critics as unhistorical or contradictory to known facts... Yet archaeological discoveries have shown that these critical charges... are wrong and that the Bible is trustworthy in the very statements which have been set aside as untrustworthy...We do not know of any cases where the Bible has been proved wrong." —Dr. Joseph P. Free

Archaeology's Amazing Findings
Over 25,000 archaeological finds demonstrate that the people, places, and events mentioned in the Bible are real and are accurately described. According to Dr. Nelson Glueck, "It may be stated categorically that no archaeological discovery has ever controverted a Biblical reference. Scores of archaeological findings have been made which confirm in clear outline or exact detail historical statements in the Bible. And, by the same token, proper evaluation of Biblical descriptions has often led to amazing discoveries."

Archaeology Corroborates the Bible
Following the 1993 discovery in Israel of a stone containing the inscriptions "House of David" and "King of Israel," *Time* magazine stated, "This writing—dated to the 9th century BC, only a century after David's reign—described a victory by a neighboring king over the Israelites... The skeptics' claim that David never existed is now hard to defend." —*Time* (December 18, 1995)

"During the past four decades, spectacular discoveries have produced data corroborating the historical backdrop of the Gospels. In 1968, for example, the skeletal remains of a crucified man were found in a burial cave in northern Jerusalem... There was evidence that his wrists may have been pierced with  nails. The knees had been doubled up and turned sideways and an iron nail (still lodged in the heel bone of one foot) driven through both heels. The shinbones appeared to have been broken, perhaps corroborating the Gospel of John." —Jeffery L. Sheler, "Is the Bible True?" *Reader's Digest* (June 2000)

Archaeology Confirms the Hittite Empire

The Scriptures make more than forty references to the great Hittite Empire. However, until one hundred years ago there was no archaeological evidence to substantiate the biblical claim that the Hittites existed. Skeptics declared that the Bible was in error, until suddenly their mouths were stopped. In 1906, Hugo Winckler uncovered a huge library of 10,000 clay tablets, which completely documented the lost Hittite Empire. We now know that at its height, the Hittite civilization rivaled Egypt and Assyria in its glory and power.

Excavations Confirm the Bible

A hidden burial chamber, dating to the first century, was discovered in 1990 two miles from the Temple

Mount. One bore the bones of a man in his sixties, with the inscription "Yehosef bar Qayafa"—meaning "Joseph, son of Caiaphas." Experts believe this was Caiaphas, the high priest of Jerusalem, who was involved in the arrest of Jesus, interrogated Him, and handed Him over to Pontius Pilate for execution.

A few decades earlier, excavations at Caesarea Maritama, the ancient seat of Roman government in Judea, uncovered a stone slab whose complete inscription may have read: "Pontius Pilate, the prefect of Judea, has dedicated to the people of Caesarea a temple in honor of Tiberius."

The discovery is truly significant, establishing that the man depicted in the Gospels as Judea's Roman governor had the authority ascribed to him by the Gospel writers. —Jeffery L. Sheler, "Is the Bible True?" *Reader's Digest* (June 2000)

11

The Bible's Historical Accuracy

The Bible's Historical Accuracy

"Given the large portion of the New Testament written by him, it's extremely significant that Luke has been established to be a scrupulously accurate historian, even in the smallest details. One prominent archaeologist carefully examined Luke's references to thirty-two countries, fifty-four cities, and nine islands, finding not a single mistake." —John McRay

History Attests to Scripture

Jesus was very precise about the destruction of the temple, saying, "Do you not see all these things? Assuredly, I say to you, not one stone shall be left here upon another, that shall not be thrown down" (Matthew 24:2; see also Luke 21:6). Why was He so specific about stones? Historian Josephus wrote of the temple's destruction by Romans in AD 70: "They carried away every stone of the sacred temple, partially in a frenzied search for every last piece of the gold ornamentation melted in the awful heat of the fire. They then plowed the ground level, and since it had already been sown with its defenders' blood, they sowed it with salt." —Josephus, *The Wars of the Jews*

Historian Attests to the Account of Jesus

"About this time there lived Jesus, a wise man, if indeed one ought to call him a man. For he was one who wrought surprising feats and was a teacher of such people as accepted the truth gladly. He won over many Jews and many Greeks. He was the Christ. When Pilate, upon hearing him accused by men of the highest standing among us, had condemned him to be crucified, those who had in the first place come to love him did not give up their affection for him. On the third day he appeared to them restored to life, for the prophets of God had prophesied these and countless other marvelous things about him. And the tribe of Christians, so called after him, has still to this day not disappeared." —Josephus, *Testimonium Flavianum*

The Bible's Harmony Attests to Its Inspiration

"The authors, speaking under the inspiration of the Holy Spirit . . . wrote on hundreds of controversial subjects with absolute harmony from the beginning to the end. There is one unfolding story from Genesis to Revelation: the redemption of mankind through the Messiah—the Old Testament through the coming Messiah, the New Testament from the Messiah that has come. In Genesis, you have paradise lost, in Revelation you have paradise gained. You can't understand Revelation without understanding Genesis. It's all interwoven on hundreds of controversial subjects.

"Now here's the picture: 1,600 years, 60 generations, 40-plus authors, different walks of life, different places, different times, different moods, different continents, three languages, writing on hundreds of controversial subjects and yet when they are brought together, there is absolute harmony from beginning to end... There is no other book in history to even compare to the uniqueness of this continuity." —Josh McDowell

12

Evolution and the Bible

If you have read through this book with an open mind, you may be wondering how the theory of evolution is compatible with the Bible. The answer is that it's not. They are diametrically opposed to one another. If evolution is true, then the Bible is false. This is because the Bible says that every animal brings forth after its own kind, while evolution says all life evolved from a common ancestor. The Bible says that there is one kind of flesh of beasts and another kind of flesh of man. In other words, man is not just another animal in the evolutionary chain.

Note that the small adaptations within a kind (such as the variety among dogs) is sometimes known as "microevolution"—although nothing new actually comes into being ("evolves"). Despite their incredible differences, dogs are still dogs.

The belief that man evolved from primates is based on "macroevolution," commonly known as "the theory of evolution." However, there is no scientific evidence for "macroevolution"—the inference that the small changes seen in adaptation can accumulate and lead to large changes over long periods. In macroevolution, one kind of creature (such as a reptile) supposedly becomes another kind of creature (such as a bird), requiring the creation of entirely new features and body types.

We are continually told that evolution is scientific, that it is a proven fact, and that the Bible is merely a collection of myths. However, strange though it may sound, it is evolution that is a collection of myths and the Bible that is a proven fact. Do you find that hard to believe? Then stay with me...

Philosophy Professor Convinced

In reference to creation, Derek Prince said, "I am simple-minded enough to believe that it happened the way the Bible described it. I have been a professor at Britain's largest university [Cambridge] for nine years. I hold various degrees and academic distinctions, and I feel in many ways I am quite sophisticated intellectually, but I don't feel in any way intellectually inferior when I say that I believe the Bible record of creation.

"Prior to believing the Bible I have studied many other attempts to explain man's origin and found them all unsatisfying and in many cases self-contradictory. I turned to study the Bible as a professional philosopher—not as a believer—and I commented to myself, 'At least it can't be any sillier than some of the other things I've heard,' and to my astonishment, I discovered it had the answer."

Evolution: Fact or Fiction?

Evolution, on the other hand, seems to supply more questions than answers.

If every creature evolved with no Creator, there are numerous problems for "scientific" evolution. Take for instance the first bird. Did the bird breathe? Did it breathe before it evolved lungs? How did it do this? Why did it evolve lungs if it was happily surviving without them? How did it know what needed to be evolved if its brain hadn't yet evolved? Did the bird have a mouth? How did it eat before it had evolved a mouth? Where did the mouth send the food before a stomach evolved? How did the bird have energy if it didn't eat (because it didn't yet have a mouth)? How did the bird see what there was to eat before its eyes evolved? Evolution is intellectual suicide. It is an embarrassment.

Professor Louis Bounoure, Director of Research, National Center of Scientific Research, so rightly stated: "Evolution is a fairy tale for grown-ups. This theory has helped nothing in the progress of science. It is useless."

Michael Ruse wrote, "An increasing number of scientists, most particularly a growing number of evolutionists ... argue that Darwinian evolutionary theory is no genuine scientific theory at all ... Many of the critics have the highest intellectual credentials." —"Darwin's Theory: An Exercise in Science," *New Scientist* (June 25, 1981)

Dr. T. N. Tahmisian of the Atomic Energy Commission said, "Scientists who go about teaching that evolution is a fact of life are great con-men, and the story they are telling may be the greatest hoax ever."

Malcolm Muggeridge, British journalist and philosopher said, "I myself am convinced that the theory of evolution, especially the extent to which it has been applied, will be one of the great jokes in the history books of the future. Posterity will marvel that so flimsy and dubious an hypothesis could be accepted with the incredible credulity that it has."

The Evolution of the Theory

Let's look at how the theory of man's evolution has evolved through the years:

"Charles Dawson, a British lawyer and amateur geologist, announced in 1912 his discovery of pieces of a human skull and an apelike jaw in a gravel pit near the town of Piltdown, England ... Dawson's announcement stopped the scorn cold. Experts instantly declared Piltdown Man (estimated to be 300,000 to one million years old) the evolutionary find of the century. Darwin's missing link had been identified.

"Or so it seemed for the next 40 or so years. Then, in the early fifties ... scientists began to suspect misattribution. In 1953, that suspicion gave way to a full-blown scandal: Piltdown Man was a hoax. Radiocarbon tests proved that its skull belonged to a 600-year old woman, and its jaw to a 500-year-old orangutan from the East Indies." —*Our Times: The Illustrated History of the 20th Century*

76

The Piltdown Man fraud wasn't an isolated incident. Many alleged "missing links" are based on only a single fossil fragment and the wishful thinking of evolutionists. The famed Nebraska Man was derived from a single tooth, which was later found to be from an extinct pig. Java Man, found in the early 20th century, was nothing more than a piece of skull, a fragment of a thigh bone, and three molar teeth. The rest came from the deeply fertile imaginations of plaster of Paris workers. Java Man is now regarded as fully human.

Heidelberg Man came from a jawbone, a large chin section, and a few teeth. Most scientists reject the jawbone because it's similar to that of modern man. Still, many evolutionists believe that he's 250,000 years old. No doubt they pinpointed his birthday with carbon dating. However, *Time* magazine (June 11, 1990) published a science article subtitled "Geologists show that carbon dating can be way off." And don't look to Neanderthal Man for any evidence of evolution. He died of exposure. His skull was exposed as being fully human, not ape. Not only was his stooped posture found to be caused by disease, but he spoke and was artistic and religious.

Dr. Colin Patterson, senior paleontologist at the British Museum of Natural History, gave a keynote address at the American Museum of Natural History, New York City, in 1981. In it, he explained his sudden "anti-evolutionary" view:

One morning I woke up and...it struck me that I had been working on this stuff for twenty years and there was not one thing I knew about it. That's quite a shock to learn that one can be misled so long...I've tried putting a simple question to various people: "Can you tell me anything you know about evolution, any one thing, any one thing that is true?" I tried that question on the geology staff at the Field Museum of Natural History and the only answer I got was silence. I tried it on the members of the Evolutionary Morphology Seminar in the University of Chicago, a very prestigious body of evolutionists, and all I got there was silence for a long time and eventually one person said, "I do know one thing—it ought not to be taught in high school."

The Religion of Evolution

If there is no evidence for evolution, why is the theory promoted so vehemently? H. S. Lipson, professor of physics, University of Manchester, UK, said, "In fact, evolution became in a sense a scientific religion; almost all scientists have accepted it and many are prepared to 'bend' their observations to fit in with it."

Professor Lipson is right. Evolution is a religion. Let's look at how people become "believers." Someone shared his faith in evolution with an unbeliever, who in time came to believe in the theory. He didn't have to turn from sin. He merely had to give up his belief in biblical creation. We may marvel at the Mormons for their simplistic belief in Joseph Smith's missing golden tablets, but the evolutionist is just as gullible. He believes without a shred of evidence. His beliefs aren't in missing gold tablets, but in the "missing link." No missing link has been found, but the evolutionist is convinced that it is there, somewhere.

Rejection of the Bible's account of creation as given in the Book of Genesis could rightly be called "Genecide," because it eradicated man's purpose of existence and left a whole generation with no certainty as to its beginning. Consequently, theories and tales of our origin have crept like primeval slime from the minds of those who don't know God. This intellectual genocide has given the godless a temporary license to labor to the extremes of their imagination, giving birth to painful conjecture of human beginnings. They speak in *speculation*, the uncertain language of those who drift aimlessly across the endless sea of secular philosophy.

The Scriptures, on the other hand, deal only with truth and certainty. They talk of fact, reality, and purpose for man's existence. The darkness of the raging sea of futility retreats where the lighthouse of Genesis begins.

Never-Changing Bible, Ever-Changing Science
According to an NBC News report in August 1999, there was a "remarkable" discovery in Australia. The *Journal of Science* reported that they had found what they considered to be proof that life appeared on earth 2.7 billion years ago—a billion years earlier than previously thought. They now admit that they were

wrong in their first estimate (a mere 1,000,000,000 years off), but with this discovery they are now sure that they have the truth ... until their next discovery.

CBS News reported in October 1999 that discoveries were made of the bones of an unknown animal in Asia that may be as much as 40 million years old. This changed scientific minds as to *where* man first originated. Scientists once believed that primates evolved in Africa, but now they think they may be wrong, and that man's ancestors may have originated in Asia. So they believe ... until the next discovery.

USA Today (March 21, 2001) reported, "Paleontologists have discovered a new skeleton in the closet of human ancestry that is likely to force science to revise, if not scrap, current theories of human origins." Reuters reported that the discovery left "scientists of human evolution ... *confused*," saying, "Lucy may not even be a direct human ancestor after all."

Charles Spurgeon said, "We are invited, brethren, most earnestly to go away from the old-fashioned belief of our forefathers because of the supposed discoveries of science. What is science? The method by which man tries to hide his ignorance. It should not be so, but so it is. You are not to be dogmatical in theology, my brethren, it is wicked; but for scientific men it is the correct thing. You are never to assert anything very strongly; but scientists may boldly assert what they cannot prove, and may demand a faith far more credulous than any we possess. Forsooth, you and I are to take our Bibles and shape and mould our belief according to the ever-shifting teachings of so-called scientific men. What folly is this!

"Why, the march of science, falsely so called, through the world may be traced by exploded fallacies and abandoned theories. Former explorers once adored are now ridiculed; the continual wreckings of false hypotheses is a matter of universal notoriety. You may tell where the supposed learned have encamped by the debris left behind of suppositions and theories as plentiful as broken bottles."

The Big Bang and Genesis

Try to think of any explosion that has produced order. Does a terrorist bomb create harmony? Big bangs cause chaos. How could a Big Bang produce a rose, apple trees, fish, sunsets, the seasons, hummingbirds, polar bears—thousands of birds and animals, each with its own eyes, nose, and mouth?

Try this interesting experiment: Empty your garage of every piece of metal, wood, paint, rubber, and plastic. *Make sure there is nothing there.* Nothing. Then wait for 10 years and see if a Mercedes evolves. Try it. If it doesn't appear, leave it for 20 years. If that doesn't work, try it for 100 years. Then try leaving it for 10,000 years. Admittedly, it is pretty hard to believe that it could appear.

However, here's what will produce the necessary blind faith to make the evolutionary process believable: leave it for 250 million years.

81

"Missing Link" Still Missing

"Did dinos soar? Imaginations certainly took flight over *Archaeoraptor Liaoningensis*, a birdlike fossil with a meat-eater's tail that was spirited out of northeastern China, 'discovered' at a Tucson, Arizona, gem and mineral show last year, and displayed at the National Geographic Society in Washington, DC. Some 110,000 visitors saw the exhibit, which closed January 17; millions more read about the find in November's *National Geographic*. Now, paleontologists are eating crow. Instead of 'a true missing link' connecting dinosaurs to birds, the specimen appears to be a composite, its unusual appendage likely tacked on by a Chinese farmer, not evolution.

"*Archaeoraptor* is hardly the first 'missing link' to snap under scrutiny. In 1912, fossil remains of an ancient hominid were found in England's Piltdown quarries and quickly dubbed man's ape-like ancestor. It took decades to reveal the hoax." —*U.S. News & World Report* (February 14, 2000)

"Darwin admitted that millions of 'missing links,' transitional life forms, would have to be discovered in the fossil record to prove the accuracy of his theory that all species had gradually evolved by chance mutation into new species. Unfortunately for his theory, despite hundreds of millions spent on searching for fossils worldwide for more than a century, the scientists have failed to locate a single missing link out of the millions that must exist if their theory of evolution is to be vindicated." —Grant R. Jeffery, *The Signature of God*

"There are gaps in the fossil graveyard, places where there should be intermediate forms, but where there is nothing whatsoever instead. No paleontologist... denies that this is so. It is simply a fact. Darwin's theory and the fossil record are in conflict." —David Berlinsky

Time magazine reported, "Scientists concede that their most cherished theories are based on embarrassingly few fossil fragments and that huge gaps exist in the fossil record" (November 7, 1977). G. K. Chesterton rightly stated, "The evolutionists seem to know everything about the missing link except the fact that it is missing."

Carbon Dating and the Fossil Record

"Radiometric dating was the culminating factor that led to the belief in billions of years for earth history. But did you know that the results from some radiometric dating methods completely undermine those from other radiometric methods? One example is carbon-14 dating. As long as an organism is alive it takes in carbon-14; however, when it dies, the carbon intake stops. Since carbon-14 is radioactive (decays into nitrogen), the amount present in a dead organism decreases over time. The amount of carbon-14 remaining can be used to date samples which were once alive, such as wood or bone.

"Carbon-14 has a half-life of 5,730 years, so any carbon-14 in organic material supposedly 100,000 years old should all have decayed into nitrogen. Some things, such as wood trapped in lava flows, said to be millions of years old by other radiometric dating methods still contain carbon-14. If the items were really millions of years old, then they should not have any traces of carbon-14 left.

"Coal and diamonds, which are found in or sandwiched between rock layers allegedly millions or billions of years old, have been shown to have carbon-14 ages of only tens of thousands of years. So which date, if any, is correct? The diamonds or coal cannot be millions of years old if they have any traces of carbon-14 still in them. The carbon-14 results show that these dating methods are completely unreliable and that the assumptions they are based on are erroneous." —Answers in Genesis

"Shells from *living* snails were carbon dated as being 27,000 years old." —*Science* magazine (vol. 224, 1984, emphasis added)

Ronald R. West, PhD, said, "Contrary to what most scientists write, the fossil record does not support the Darwinian theory of evolution because it is this theory (there are several)  which we use to interpret the fossil record. By doing so we are guilty of circular reasoning if we then say the fossil record supports this theory."

Evolution and Irreducible Complexity

In his book *Darwin's Black Box*, biochemistry professor Michael J. Behe, an evolutionist, acknowledges a "powerful challenge to Darwinian evolution"—something he refers to as "irreducible complexity." He gives a simple example: the humble mousetrap. The mousetrap has five major components that make it functional. If any one of these components is missing, it will not function. It becomes worthless as a mousetrap.

He explains that an irreducibly complex system cannot be produced by slight, successive modifications, "because any precursor to an irreducibly complex system that is missing a part is by definition nonfunctional . . . Since natural selection can only choose systems that are already working, then if a biological system cannot be produced gradually it would have to arise as an integrated unit, in one fell swoop, for natural selection to have anything to act on."

Charles Darwin admitted, "If it could be demonstrated that any complex organ existed which could not possibly have been formed by numerous, successive, slight modifications, my theory would absolutely break down" (*The Origin of Species*).

If we just take the human eye, one small part of an incredibly complex creation, we will see this same principle of irreducible complexity. The eye cannot be reduced to anything less than what it is. It has thousands of co-equal functions to make it work. If we take away just one of those functions, the rest of the eye is worthless as an eye. How then did the eye evolve when all functions had to be present at once to give it any worth at all?

"To suppose that the eye, with all its inimitable contrivances for adjusting the focus to different distances, for admitting different amounts of light, and for the correction of spherical and chromatic aberration, could have been formed by natural selection,

 seems, I freely confess, absurd in the highest degree." —Charles Darwin, *The Origin of Species*

(No wonder—the focusing muscles in the eye move an estimated 100,000 times each day. The retina contains 137 million light-sensitive cells.)

Evolution and the Earth's Population

"The evolutionary scientists who believe that man existed for over a million years have an almost insurmountable problem. Using the assumption of forty-three years for an average human generation, the population growth over a million years would produce 23,256 consecutive generations. We calculate the expected population by starting with one couple one million years ago and use the same assumptions of a forty-three-year generation and 2.5 children per family... The evolutionary theory of a million years of growth would produce trillions × trillions × trillions × trillions of people that should be alive today on our planet. To put this in perspective, this number is vastly greater than the total number of atoms in our vast universe.

"If mankind had lived on earth for a million years, we would all be standing on enormously high mountains of bones from the trillions of skeletons of those who had died in past generations. However,

despite the tremendous archeological and scientific investigation in the last two centuries, the scientists have not found a fraction of the trillions of skeletons predicted by the theory of evolutionary scientists."
—Grant R. Jeffery, *The Signature of God*

The Bible and Blood

Platelets play an important role in preventing the loss of blood by beginning a chain reaction that results in blood clotting. As blood begins to flow from a cut or scratch, platelets respond to help the blood clot and to stop the bleeding after a short time.

Platelets promote the clotting process by clumping together and forming a plug at the site of a wound and then releasing proteins called "clotting factors." These proteins start a series of chemical reactions that are extremely complicated. Every step of the clotting must go smoothly if a clot is to form. If one of the clotting factors is missing or defective, the clotting process does not work. A serious genetic disorder known as "hemophilia" results from a defect in one of the clotting factor genes. Because they lack one of the clotting factors, hemophilia sufferers may bleed uncontrollably from even small cuts or scrapes.

To form a blood clot there must be twelve specific individual chemical reactions in our blood. If evolution is true, and if this twelve-step process didn't happen in the first generation (i.e., if any one of these specific reactions failed to operate in their exact function and order), no creatures would have survived. They all would have bled to death!

Fossil Evidence Points to Genesis Account

"The creation account in Genesis and the theory of evolution could not be reconciled. One must be right and the other wrong. The story of the fossils agrees with the account of Genesis. In the oldest rocks we did not find a series of fossils covering the gradual changes from the most primitive creatures to developed forms but rather, in the oldest rocks, developed species suddenly appeared. Between every species there was a complete absence of intermediate fossils."
—D. B. Gower (biochemist), "Scientist Rejects Evolution," *Kentish Times*

Based on all the evidence, Professor H. S. Lipson concludes: "We must...admit that the only acceptable explanation is creation. I know this is anathema to physicists, as indeed it is to me, but we must not reject a theory that we do not like if the experimental evidence supports it."

13

Science and Evolution

Evolution is actually a religion. The *Funk & Wagnall* dictionary defines "religion" as "a set of beliefs concerned with explaining the origins and purposes of the universe." That sums up the religion of evolution. It even has its own religious language: "We believe, perhaps, maybe, probably, could've, possibly." The founding father of the faith is Charles Darwin. The god of the religion of evolution is "nature," often referred to by the faithful as "Mother Nature." Listen to how they give her praise.

She is responsible for everything we can see in creation. What's more, Mother Nature is a deaf, blind mute. She doesn't hear anything, she doesn't see anything, and most importantly—she doesn't *say* anything. Mother Nature doesn't have any moral dictates. That's why evolution is so appealing. This is called "idolatry," and is a transgression of the First of the Ten Commandments. Evolution doesn't disprove the existence of God. It just reveals that those who believe it are truly capable of faith in the invisible. All it takes to believe is a great leap of blind faith. Like little children, evolutionists believe without the need of a shred of evidence. They confirm Napoleon's observation: "Man will believe anything, as long as it's not in the Bible."

Faith vs. Evidence

Perhaps you are convinced that the Bible is supernatural, and you have seen that evolution is an unproven, unscientific theory. It is merely a belief. Perhaps you think that believing in God is also a matter of "faith." Not so.

When I look at a building, how do I know that there was a builder? I can't see him, hear him, touch, taste, or smell him. Of course, the build*ing* is proof that there was a build*er*. In fact, I couldn't want better evidence that there was a builder than to have the building in front of me. I don't need "faith" to know that there was a builder. All I need are eyes that can see and a brain that works. Likewise, when I look at a painting, how can I know that there was a painter? Again, the paint*ing* is proof positive that there was a paint*er*. I don't need "faith" to believe in a painter because I can see the clear evidence.

The same principle applies with the existence of God. When I look at creation, how can I *know* that there was a Creator? I can't see Him, hear Him, touch, taste, or smell Him. How can I know that He exists? Why, creation shows me that there is a Creator. *I couldn't want better proof that a Creator exists than to have the fact of creation in front of me.* I don't need faith to believe in a Creator; all I need are eyes that can see and a brain that works: "For since the creation of the world His invisible attributes are clearly seen, being understood by the things that are made, even His eternal power and Godhead, so that they are without excuse" (Romans 1:20).

If, however, I want the builder to *do* something for me, *then* I need to have faith in him. The same applies to God: "Without faith it is impossible to please Him, for he who comes to God must believe that He is, and that He is a rewarder of those who diligently seek Him" (Hebrews 11:6).

Sir Isaac Newton once said, "This most beautiful system of the sun, planets, and comets could only proceed from the counsel and dominion of an intelligent and powerful Being."

Louis Pasteur said, "The more I study nature, the more I stand amazed at the work of the Creator." Evolutionist Stephen Hawking wrote, "It would be very difficult to explain why the universe should have begun in just this way, except as the act of a God who intended to create beings like us" (*A Brief History of Time*). He also stated: "Then we shall ... be able to take part in the discussion of the question of why it is that we and the universe exist. If we find the answer to that, it would be the ultimate triumph of human reason—for then we would know the mind of God."

The Mind of God

We can get a glimpse of the incredible mind of God simply by looking at His creation. Take one (very) small part—the mind of man: The brain is a soft lump of tissue weighing about 3 pounds. It is one of the most watery organs of the body, its outer tissue being 85 percent water. There is very little relationship between brain size and intelligence. Some very bright people have smaller brains than those who are less intelligent. The brain feels no pain because it has no pain receptors. It floats in fluid inside the skull, and the fluid (derived from blood) acts as a shock absorber. The brain stops growing in size at about age 15.

Its surface is covered with folds. If it were laid out flat, the brain surface would cover two average student desks. The brain has four times as many nerve cells as there are people on earth. With its 10 billion neurons, it can record 86 million bits of information each day of our lives. Supporting, protecting, and nourishing these 10 billion neurons are 100 billion glia cells, which make up half the mass of the brain. Since nerve cells can't reproduce, you have fewer of them as you get older. Persons of 70 or 80 may have only 75 percent of the nerve cells they were born with.

Nerve impulses travel more quickly than cars do, with some up to 250 miles per hour. If all the nerves were laid end to end, they would stretch almost 45 miles. If all the nerve cell connections—axons and dendrites—from a human brain were placed end to end, they would encircle the earth many times. The dendrites alone could stretch about 100,000 miles.

Let's now look to the heavens: "They defined the exact shape of the closest major galaxy, a beautiful spiral named Andromeda, containing more than 300 billion stars. The nearest of these is (an incredible) thirteen quintillion (13,000,000,000,000,000,000) miles, or 2.2 million light-years, beyond the Milky Way, a distance calculated by comparing the star's apparent brightness with a star of similar brightness and known distance from Earth. And beyond Andromeda lay billions of other galaxies." —*Solar System* (Time-Life Books).

The incredible complexity of the human brain and the vastness of the heavens speak of the awesome power of the Creator's mind, and together "declare the glory of God" (Psalm 19:1).

The Bible Gives the Reason for Suffering

Study the soil for a moment. It naturally produces weeds. No one plants them; no one waters them. They even stubbornly push through cracks of a dry sidewalk. Millions of useless weeds sprout like there's no tomorrow, strangling our crops and ruining our lawns. Pull them out by the roots, and there will be more tomorrow. They are nothing but a curse!

Consider how much of the earth is uninhabitable. There are millions of square miles of barren deserts in Africa and other parts of the world. Most of Australia is nothing but miles and miles of useless desolate land. Not only that, but the earth is constantly shaken with massive earthquakes. Its shores are lashed with hurricanes; tornadoes rip through creation with incredible fury; devastating floods soak the land; and terrible droughts parch the soil. Sharks, tigers, lions, snakes, spiders, and disease-carrying mosquitoes attack humanity and suck its life's blood.

The earth's inhabitants are afflicted with disease, pain, suffering, and death. Think of how many people are plagued with cancer, Alzheimer's, multiple sclerosis, heart disease, emphysema, Parkinson's, and a number of other debilitating illnesses. Consider all the children with leukemia, or people born with crippling diseases or without the mental capability to even feed themselves. All these things should convince thinking minds that something is radically wrong. Did God blow it when He created humanity? What sort of tyrant must our Creator be if this was His master plan? Sadly, many use the issue of suffering as an excuse to reject any thought of God, when its existence is the *very reason* we should accept Him. Suffering stands as terrible testimony to the truth of the explanation given by the Word of God.

The Bible tells us that God cursed the earth because of Adam's transgression. Weeds *are* a curse. So is disease. Sin and suffering cannot be separated. The Scriptures inform us that we live in a *fallen* creation. In the beginning, God created man perfect, and he lived in a perfect world without suffering. *It was heaven on earth*.

When sin came into the world, death and misery came with it. Those who understand the message of Holy Scripture eagerly await a new heaven and a new earth "in which righteousness dwells." In that coming

Kingdom there will be no more pain, suffering, disease, or death. We are told that no eye has ever seen, nor has any ear heard, neither has any man's mind ever imagined the wonderful things that God has in store for those who love Him (1 Corinthians 2:9).

Think for a moment what it would be like if food grew with the fervor of weeds. Consider how wonderful it would be if the deserts became incredibly fertile, if creation stopped devouring humanity. Imagine if the weather worked *for* us instead of against us, if disease completely disappeared, if pain was a thing of the past, if death was no more.

The dilemma is that we are like a child whose insatiable appetite for chocolate has caused his face to break out with ugly sores. He looks in the mirror and sees a sight that makes him depressed. But instead of giving up his beloved chocolate, he consoles himself by stuffing more into his mouth. Yet the source of his pleasure is actually the *cause* of his suffering. The whole face of the earth is nothing but ugly sores of suffering. Everywhere we look we see unspeakable pain. But instead of believing God's explanation and asking Him to forgive us and change our appetite, we run deeper into sin's sweet embrace. There we find solace in its temporal pleasures, thus intensifying our pain, both in this life and in the life to come.

The Bible Gives the Reason for Death
The Scriptures answer questions that science cannot. It tells us why we die and how each of us can conquer the power of death.

Before we look at the Bible's explanation, let me ask you a question. How many unsolved murder cases ("perfect" crimes) do you think there were in the United States between 1990 and 2000? Take a guess: A) 2,410; B) 31; or C) 100,000?

Probably most would say 31. Some, with a little more insight, would say 2,410. However, the correct answer is C. Over 100,000 people were shot, strangled, stabbed, or poisoned and no one was brought to justice.[2] If your loved one were one of the victims, you would no doubt be outraged by such injustice. It would then make sense to you that there would be final justice for those murderers on the Day of Judgment. C. S. Lewis said, "There is no doctrine which I would more willingly remove from Christianity than the doctrine of hell, if it lay in my power. But it has the full support of Scripture and, especially, of our Lord's own words; it has always been held by the Christian Church, and it has the support of reason." In light of heinous crimes, a place called "hell" makes sense. God should not, cannot, *will* not let murderers go free.

However, the Bible warns that He will be very thorough on the Day of Judgment. You may not be a murderer, but here's a checklist of the Ten Commandments to see if you should be worried:

Have you ever lied (even once—fibs, white lies, etc.)? Ever stolen anything (the value is irrelevant)? Jesus said, "Whoever looks at a woman to lust for her

---

[2] Approximately 22,000 homicides yearly. National average resolution 51 percent.

has already committed adultery with her in his heart." Have you ever looked with lust? If you have said "Yes" to these three questions, by your own admission, you are a  lying, thieving adulterer at heart, and we've only looked at three of the Ten Commandments.

That's how God sees you. Nothing is hidden from His holy eyes. You have to face all Ten Commandments on that Day. Do you think that you will you be innocent or guilty on the Day of Judgment? Listen to your conscience. You know that you will be guilty, and therefore end up in hell. That's not God's will. He provided a way for you to be forgiven. The "wages of sin is death," but He sent His Son to take your punishment: "God demonstrates His own love toward us, in that while we were still sinners, Christ died for us." All of the sins of the world were laid on Him as He hung on a Roman cross. He was "bruised" for our iniquities when He suffered and died in our place. Then three days later, Jesus rose from the dead and defeated death. There is no other name under heaven whereby we must be saved. Only Jesus can forgive sins—no religion, no prophet, no good works (which are an attempt to bribe God). Cry out to God to forgive you, repent (turn from all sin), and put your trust in Jesus Christ alone (the same way you would trust a parachute to save you).

Through the cross of Calvary, Almighty God offers you the gift of everlasting life. Is that a good deal?

Think about it for a moment. *You are going to die.* It may be in twenty years; it may be tonight. What then are you waiting for? Don't let petty issues or your love for sin take you to hell. Please, confess and forsake your sins right now. If you don't know how to do that, pray something like this:

> Dear God, please forgive my sins (name them). I repent of every sin I have ever committed. I thank you that Jesus took my punishment and rose again on the third day. I now put my trust in Him to be my Lord and my Savior. In Jesus' name I pray.

Now read the Bible daily and obey what you read. God will never let you down.

~

Thank you for taking the time to read this book. Much of this material was taken from *The Evidence Study Bible* (Bridge-Logos), which contains a wealth of additional evidences for the truth of the Bible.

Resources

If you have not yet placed your trust in Jesus Christ and would like additional information, please check out the following helpful resources:

How to Know God Exists: Scientific Proof of God. Clear evidences for His existence will convince you that belief in God is reasonable and rational—a matter of fact and not faith.

Made In Heaven. Discover how the most innovative ideas of modern human ingenuity are actually features borrowed from the amazing work of God in creation.

Why Christianity? (DVD). If you have ever asked what happens after we die, if there is a Heaven, or how good we have to be to go there, this DVD will help you.

See our YouTube channel (youtube.com/livingwaters) to watch free movies such as "The Atheist Delusion," "Evolution vs. God," "Crazy Bible," as well as thousands of other fascinating videos.

If you are a new believer, please read "Save Yourself Some Pain," written just for you (available free online at LivingWaters.com, or as a booklet).

For Christians

Please visit our website where you can sign up for our free weekly e-newsletter. To learn how to share your faith the way Jesus did, don't miss these helpful resources:

- *God Has a Wonderful Plan for Your Life: The Myth of the Modern Message* (our most important book)
- *Hell's Best Kept Secret* and *True & False Conversion* (you can listen to these vital messages free at LivingWaters.com)
- *Basic Training Course* (evangelism DVD study)
- *Tough Questions* (apologetics DVD study)
- *Anyone But Me*
- *What Did Jesus Do?*
- *How to Bring Your Children to Christ... & Keep Them There*
- *The Way of the Master for Kids*
- *Out of the Comfort Zone*
- *World Religions in a Nutshell*

You can also gain further insights by watching the *Way of the Master* television program (Wayofthe Master.com).

For more resources, visit LivingWaters.com, call 800-437-1893, or write to: Living Waters Publications, P.O. Box 1172, Bellflower, CA 90707.

THE EVIDENCE STUDY BIBLE

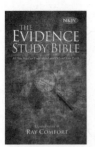

"An invaluable tool for becoming a more effective witness."
—FRANKLIN GRAHAM

The Evidence Study Bible arms you not just with apologetic information to refute the arguments of skeptics, but with practical evangelism training on how to lead them to Christ.

- Discover answers to over 200 questions such as: Why is there suffering? Where did Cain get his wife? How could a loving God send people to hell? What about those who never hear of Jesus?

- In addition to thousands of verse-related comments, over 130 informative articles will help you better comprehend and communicate the Christian faith.

- Over two dozen articles on evolution will thoroughly prepare you to refute the theory.

- Dozens of articles on other religions will help you understand and address the beliefs of Mormons, Hindus, Muslims, Jehovah's Witnesses, cults, etc.

- Hundreds of inspiring quotes from renowned Christian leaders and practical tips on defending your faith will greatly encourage and equip you.

The Evidence Study Bible provides powerful and compelling evidence that will enrich your trust in God and His Word, deepen your love for the truth, and enable you to reach those you care about with the message of eternal life.